LEAVING HOWE ISLAND

LEAVING

HOWE

ISLAND

by Sadiqa de Meijer

OOLICHAN BOOKS
FERNIE, BRITISH COLUMBIA, CANADA
2013

Library and Archives Canada Cataloguing in Publication

De Meijer, Sadiqa, 1977-, author

    Leaving Howe Island / Sadiqa de Meijer.

ISBN 978-0-88982-295-5 (pbk.)

    I. Title.

PS8607.E523L43 2013   C811'.6   C2013-905853-2

We gratefully acknowledge the financial support of the Canada Council for the Arts, the British Columbia Arts Council through the BC Ministry of Tourism, Culture, and the Arts, and the Government of Canada through the Book Publishing Industry Development Program, for our publishing activities.

Published by
Oolichan Books
P.O. Box 2278
Fernie, British Columbia
Canada V0B 1M0

www.oolichan.com

for my daughter

and in memory of Beppe

'K maak in gedachten vaak een bedevaart

- J.A. dèr Mouw

In thought I often make a pilgrimage

Contents

Great Aunt Unmarried

There, There

Great Aunt Unmarried

Great Aunt Unmarried

i.

The past, because
look at the binoculars:
massive, grained, a leather strap.

Her vision, handed over,
is an underwater blur.

Subsidized flat a crow's nest.

Custard and orange rations, anagram games.

Below orchestral radio, the elevator's pitch. Gulls
shear the view.

A freighter first is a shimmer, a possible snag in the seam.

Schip! Smudge of form,
distilling contours, sea as Polaroid. We love
the tempera colours of hulls, sightless surrenders
to tugboats, Russians for their stately,
intergalactic names.

ii.

Freighters marvellous as whales, moored under the smokestack
forest of the smelters. Saffron chimney flame a nightlight
in calico curtains, woollen sunrises. That sleep dust
drowsing our eyes was soot, those ore ships were
dismantling the earth, but who in ladybug sneakers,
who in orthopedic loafers wouldn't speed
to the gorge of the locks, wave at sailors tossing ropes
across the churning chasm between hull and us?
Home with herring from a harbour truck, we watched them move
upstream, year after booming year. Freighters dwarfing
row houses, slow embolisms in the bloodstream
of our patchwork landscape, rivers mapped
to the veins of our wrists.

iii.

After the dune road,
vast beach of damp sand, sparsely
peopled, dogged.

The crowds are a city south
in pavilions. You can't see England —
that's cloud, tomorrow's

duller weather. Past the kelp
threshold: soup bowl cephalopods,
crab fragments,

razor shells. I dig. Wind clatters the fabric
of flags, whips words inland.
Such quicksilver

light. Breakers, ambulant soda can.
The freighter looms impossibly
on its inch of sea.

camera, film

Three girls in salt dresses, ribbons
askew. Fierce shine on tired shoes. He's told
them to clasp hands and freeze.
Foto Modern embossed in gold.

Strandbeesten

Dunes, green shadow, rumpled blanket.

Later, who will remember roads, the wrecking balls
and scaffolds of cities.

That pinkish, parasol-shelled species congregating
on the beaches, squealing like stricken rabbits, but with pleasure.

Anchored by grasses and buckthorn, fog-frayed in the mornings.

Pulverized sea-shell trails, grinding under our bicycle wheels,
as if we had a geologic task.

I'm not sure now if there were ponies, cocoa-flanked, deft on sand slopes,
or if we drew them: a herd taped over the window's rambling view.

Also, it may have been a dream, but I thought great plastic beasts
arrived at low tide, stilt-legs synchronous as piano scales,
on the volition of the wind.

Interbellum

for I. & Z.

We are playing on sheared grass, a stubble raft, our bodies
gleaming nut wood. Scabs heal in hours. Visions
flame and fall to ash in the plastic lives
we hover over — hinged men, giraffes,
blonde doll we tilt to shut her eyes.

Someone against the viscous trembling air
is circling us, wading the deeper grass, steady
as a clock's tick, head lowered to the crisscrossed
ochre blades, the rough-edged blades rustling with hidden
insects, shrinking shadows of late morning.

In his hands, a heavy stick, raised to smash the skull
of any nearing snake. Old hands, they were, over a cook's
apron. Fingers singed at the *tawa*, grouted with flour.

Because of whom, because of whom.

camera, film

Eyes downcast and that man
beside her. Bottle of rosehip cordial.
Sundress, De Stijl, colours unknown.
Skin lit as if the flash was internal.

Bloodbottlers

In the below city,
the warren of streets and brick
playgrounds, fishmongers and butcher shops,
the over-coated grown-ups say   *your grandniece,*
                                                                so dark?

Under clouded brows they say it,
boiling their voices to treacle
clots they weigh my hair, hands barnacled
with yellowed eyeballs.

All the seabirds are on strings and lift our wondrous airship
            higher!
                        higher!
                                    but
                        upstairs, my skewed
trajectory: mirror, binoculars,
      mirror again.

Spellbound

Some evenings, after the phone-call
home, after pyjamas and making
the lit grids of buildings snake
in the lenses, I'd sprawl
on the oatmeal carpet,
reversing the binoculars.
Against the ceiling's curvature,
the lamp was a silver planet.

Or things stayed as they were —
the difference was that I was far.
Exiled, half-disappeared,
breath held. Watching her
knit in a circle framed
by darkness, the titanic
seconds almost made me sick.
I only had to speak her name.

camera, film

Upright sentinel of order among forty-three
third graders. War is over.
It's all over their faces. That boy
in breeches! That waif seeking cover.

Friesland

i.

One year we drove the long, fogged seawall
to see her sisters

in their province, which had its own language, and was known

for stoics, though it flew
a flag of hearts.

Pastures etched with narrow roads.

I saw her shrink
behind the steering wheel. A dandelion shuts for rain

like that. She spoke to me by accident

in the dialect, and blushed — *not far now,*
I guessed, a tinge

of bovine melancholy in the vowels.

Someone had stitched the earth and sky together
with dim rows of poplars.

ii.

Embedded in the strata of that visit, under the wallpaper's beige umbels,
the severe ancestors framed in ovals, deep in the woods on the hooked

tablecloth, where boars foraged knowing the musket-shots of conversation
could not strike them, the youngest sister, newly octogenarian,

pressed a rock into my hand. *Kandij*, a fragment from the dark sugar
they had stirred into their coffee. I could tell that the protocol

was to skip through the uncurling ferns, licking merrily, but I was
seventeen, already I carried a furtive notebook in the pocket where the shard

dropped, almost weightless. Their spoons with schooner handles, clinking,
and the glazed brown cups, and the round tray with a landscape.

iii.

We went for a drive in nature. Two of them tied ivory
kerchiefs around their home permanents while the third
muttered a curse on vanity, and we folded into a sedan,
automatic for the rheumatisms. At the speed of a procession,
to the dissolution of chalk peppermints. *Here,* the middle sister
nodded to the shoulder. Lawn chairs emerged. From the ditch,
the road was hearsay. Buttercups towered over a far spire.
The three in bifocals, their hands on their slacks
trembled like the grass. To the south, the air force was practising.
Whether that haunted or comforted them, I couldn't tell.
On the drive to the house, the silence had a grander shape,
like a bell that fits over fields and villages, and schoolhouses
and sugar beets and people.

camera, film

This laugh it was seismic—
no decorum could subdue it,
and eventually her dentures
would dislodge and that would renew it.

Night

Not dark. That makes it June,
or close. The curtain screens
the foliage. Downstairs,
their walks, blind signatures.
Floating in abridged beds,
sheets brittle and imbued
with backyard trees.
Even bicycles release
a sound in passing, tremulous
as insects. Awake, because
of the light. Loose thoughts
ascend to the white
ceiling: fantastic
Mr. Fox's plan, trick
knots, the voltage
in a friend's stray touch,
visions of scoring from midfield.
Each night a penciled
tracing paper, overlaid to make
one form, almost opaque.
Words below, but aimless.
I forgot to memorize their faces.
Gods of fuselage and baggage trucks.
No, gods of clocks.

Introducing the Incredible Pseudomorph

There was a classmate's father who told me
I was special.

It was at a sleepover she was very popular not everyone
was invited.

Very, very special because of my parts white and dark together.

So.

Some squid, when there is trouble, release a phantom
in their own shape.

It has to do with mucus in the ink.

And everything with everything.

sketch, pencil

The light of television. Sunk in a blank
chair, glued to the Brandenburg Gate
or Rwanda. Just before ablutions
and half a sleeping pill. Late.

Transoceanic

Calls orchestrated over the clock-warp
of Greenland, cables, constellations.

Static was a constant breaker, traversing
an endless beach.

Calvinist, so every word had to outweigh
the coin that was its counterpart, but not too nakedly.

Often delays in the line made our voices collide: I saw
a skunk do you dream under the dumpster in English now? You go.

Or another conversation crackled in the background,
obliquely urgent, on the verge of clarity.

Later, she called at odd hours, her greeting as close
as the pillow, bright as the blood-red numbers.

Some nights, she mislaid the horn.
So then it was me and the sea.

(fragment)

Seconds when she flickers
in the lantern of a stranger—
coarse eyebrows, slow douse
of a grin. I'm kinder then.

There, There

Leaving Howe Island

Evening, a downpour blurring
river, sky — ferry a cradle of cold
metal, shelterless, crests washing
insect remains from our windshield — *where
are we going?* our daughter asks
and my voice says *across*
as if I'm unsure, here on a taut
cable under the river's
origin, trees angled, slate waves
someone is knitting loose and furious —
remember where the channel opens to sloped
flanks of breaching granite, campsites,
osprey-haunted — at Prescott
the granary's shadow, dark sentry, *scraw*
of a heron, water widened
by machines and the highways
start knotting themselves, dear lady
of the harbour, what I meant
to tell you stuttered, sank —
flat stone I wouldn't know
from others on that silt edge of the tidal
fleuve where bees drone jagged
in wild rose, our daughter
gripping my skirt — that was
downriver, upstream in time, and further
out is what I first saw of this place,
miles high from a plastic
window, reading the languageless
figures, terrestrial woodcuts, a river
glittering with what should've been
potential or something and now
have I made it, the ferry
slowing, docking solid, a soaked
stranger in neon overalls
waving us on

Hush

Don't be scared. Every airplane is a suspension
of disbelief, a merger of physics and faith.

Every airplane guides its housefly tongue
along a curving, snagless line. Its corridor of earth

is lined with lights. So don't be scared:
let that crescendo of the engines be your trust

that nothing levitates on algebra alone. Subdue
the sputter of doubt. The bags are checked,

the brown men shackled to the ground; their secrets,
pulled like rotten teeth, are yours.

As is the sky, swept clean by searchlights, emptied
even of the moon, the stars.

Retrospect

Do you remember us? Tweed trousers, frays
in sequined cardigans, quaint glamour sifted from
the Clothing-for-a-Dime. We found ten dollars
in a pocket once and watched a matinee, left
bread and roses! stickers on the screens of bank machines.
Breathless games on our substrate
of adequate homes: you couldn't call us insurgents,
but that look we tried to take, through discarded
glasses, milliner feathers enlivened with dye,
shirts mended by buried hands — it gave
its own light, like a misconstrued optics diagram.
Later, the men in our lives would ask, *were you lovers?*
and we would say, *no*, which was true, because
they didn't mean, of a gesture's afterglow.

I Am a Rock / What I Am

Neighbours never guessed that we lived in a lapsed
circus, tattered canvas disguised as a row house.
Where there should have been marvels,
a circular emptiness.

I used to barricade my room. I made tapes
from radio, dial chasing the space before songs —
in that leap to record, a vestige of trapeze,
the static's swell of applause.

Imagine there has long been no audience:
the ringmaster has evicted the clowns, uncaged
the carnivores, and lurks under the bleachers,
a noise-maker in his teeth.

Maybe they knew. Possibly every home is a drywall
tent, rank with bewildered elephants,
stale popcorn. The ring
of the doorbell the signal to sweep.

When Paul Simon and Edie Brickell married, I thought
that everything would be okay. Because my mix tapes
were, between surges of static, skilled enough
to sway whoever orchestrated love.

Exhibit

This is the pink salwar kameez she made for me.
Here are the air-mailed measurements:
shoulder width and ankle cuffs. Blurred fingers
sewing sequins on slipping fabric.

This is my scowl in the photograph.
These upstairs bathroom fixtures are a witness
to arms in bleaching cream and the straw
of winter fields is my landscape.

Salwar kameez over heavy boots.
Salwar kameez as comet between car and banquet hall,
trail of rosewater coconut chemical blister —
that was on manual shutter-speed.

Here is my face in a hundred miniscule mirrors,
compound eye of classmates, strangers, satellites
and drones are cratering
my countries, I haven't been there.

Salwar kameez as costumes
on the thrift store's rack with zombie leotards
and skeletons on coat hangers. This is the sale-priced
rayon and here is my pain threshold.

These seams fasten sleeves to skin and the trajectory
of free-fall was impossible to document
because of snow. Salwar kameez as nakedness.
Salwar kameez as parachute.

There, There

Poppies are tap-rooted and do not take well to transplanting,
so sow the seeds in flowering position in early spring.

- Florabunda Seed Catalogue

Then it was April. We'd set all our clocks to the future.
It was the last of first and last, the month to ask
the liquor store for boxes. Then to suture up the past,
to set each step down like a stitch and lay
a nurse-like hand on what we'd miss. I took a spade
and scraped the dirt, shook your black cloud
into the shut sieve of my fist. Dry whispers as you shifted,
claws on branches, tongue-tied clicks, as if upon release
you'd scatter into crows. That day was rehearsal:
later, I would blink my shutter eyelids at the house and drive
as if the truck were band-aid — one clean pull —
I'd need you then, unfolding, comma of root and leaf.

Moncton Toujours en Avant

No other weather suits them; the stubborn
churches. Old men still dressed for Sunday
as the neighbourhood unravels at the sleeves.

And an army of cars rolls past them, neutral.
The city used to end here, now it creeps

outside itself. *He rains. He makes cold.*
He turns the green pastures into Sobeys,
easy. Only the sky is a steel ceiling.

Ford or Dodge, Infiniti: that last triumphant
word to end debates when we were small —

how far you could run, or how much you loved.
Fugitive, home for the funeral,
distance reconciled with gasoline.

Refugee

I want to wake up unshaken, speak like the percolator's
comfortable mutter. Instead, each night, I dream
the new neighbourhood together: how the woman
in the velvet skirt who looks like Claire
will not be Claire, how the colour
of sunflowers will land in my eyes
like punches. *Fine,* I say to the poker-faced city,
and I go outside, where things appear
deserted, but on the porches there are many
solitary people, sinking in lawn-chairs, staring out. And I walk
through the lighthouse beams of their vision, turning
corners. Then the houses give way
to a great pit, walled with wood, small, glassless windows
syncopated to my stride. And oh, the resigned
gestures of back-hoes, early in the morning,
the will to carry on.

These People

Something is going very well for them. They have
their houses with sound shingles and perimeters of grass.
The breathtaking loads of groceries, complex carriages for babies.

They keep their driveways sealed, their affections on leashes,
tugged around the block. When they falter, they're patched
with inanimate joints and molars.

You can set your clock by them. You can jog
past their deafening tools and sense that your suit
is curious. Even when their lenses darken, grow inscrutable.

Their songs are private to their ears. They shear
their conversations like their lawns, these people of the *howeryou*
without awaiting answers.

They refuse superstition, but dart
from their doors to their automobiles as if the evil eye
is in the trees. Unharmed, they wish

to mean no harm. They will, when asked for directions,
erase the ambush from their faces as if it was never there.
They are what they say; they are okay.

Because There Was and There Wasn't a City

Daydream of the homesick general
with a gourd gut. Grounds of the narrow,
beef-broth river. Expanse of barracks
and fairgrounds, cathedral malls, bright
jeeps. Namesaken, swollen town.
Copper-top towers of insurance magnates,
medical hall of fame. City of remaining
maples, snuffed neon, pensioners
ruminating over donuts.

Someone keeps the kitchen light on
for me there. The half-moons
under her eyes hold my fingerprints.
Blue boxes, black walnuts, aftermath
of skunk. A tunnel I threaded
my bike through. On summer nights,
the howls of monkeys caged in an aging
amusement park gave chase.

City, I can almost see you. City, I have
a flawed allegiance. My founding
father is the doctor mopping
classroom floors.

City of benign industries, warm gusts
of cornflakes and beer. In pauses,
the river itself — slick muck, still turtles,
rot. A volunteer on scaffolds
faithfully repaints Return To Your
Fortress, O Prisoners Of Hope.

City of my sudden lankiness, your clouds
spark with plus and minus signs,
drenching restored Victorians, forgotten
laundry, the path where my name
is an absence in a park bench.

Jewel of India

From the dim hallway, walls swollen with summer damp.

Concave threshold to the morning's livid light.

When my father said *Gerrard Street East*, his voice.

The passing subway tremors upwards, into me, reverberates in ligaments and membranes.

On canvas shoes through minor parks, a pinball in a rudderless machine.

My father, transiently animate. Funny in the ebbing language, bantering with shopkeepers.

A lifeguard pours bleach in the fractured blue wading pool, sloshes it out with her legs.

If I could, I'd view a produce stand as he did, fill a paper bag with dillweed, bitter melon, ladyfingers.

Miraculous reversal poster in the window of the Portuguese apothecary.

Who lived where he never resembled somebody.

Belled, metal restaurant elephant. They're barely open. The woman fills and seals samosas in the uproar of a standing fan.

I have tea. Father, dayflower, I keep arriving at this dead end where the menu says exotic, stamped with sickle chilies.

The fan blades clatter frantically in their cage. A ghetto-blaster spools ghazals.

Her husband, over the counter, shouts: *The pavements here are very bad. You must take your walks on the pitch, in circles. This is what all of us do.*

Our Lady of Grace

I volunteered because I'd seen a burned
and orphaned boy, on the news over my plate
of noodles. Comforting him seemed
imperative, impossible, so I convinced
myself that need is need, and maybe
someone in the dark glass levels
of the Grace was as alone.

The uniform was a green shirt-dress
and suited my fellow volunteers, brisk women
whose lipstick glared in their locker mirrors.
I was much taller, and the hemline that fell
to their knees bisected my nylon thighs.
They could make *dear* sound sharp.

There was a vacancy in Ultrasound.
I had to fill the plastic squeeze bottles with gel
and circle the waiting room, urging patients
to hold their urine. When I'd proven capable,
they had me answer the phone over breaks. I liked
proceeding from the heading on the yellow
message pad: *While You Were Out...*

There was a rumour that the Grace
was testing a robotic porter. They said
it could sense obstacles by sonar like a bat.
One afternoon, in the cooked linen smell
of the corridor, it rolled alongside me,
like R2D2 welded to a dumbwaiter, and lit
the elevator button without touch.

Other things I had tried were marches
and canvassing and once on the sidewalk
next to a gas station, I held a sheet
of bristol board that said How Many Lives

Per Gallon? in red paint, which wasn't metric
but sounded better.

Those years are half blank
to me now: what was taught in school, or how old
my parents looked — but I remember standing
beside the robot, in front of elevator doors,
waiting and waiting for an acknowledgement
of me, the hesitant, human-shaped
obstacle. Some signal of lights or beeps.

Labour Day Weekend, Lake Huron

It could have been a tide of fish eggs, if you squinted. Like a leap
year or cicadas? And then gorging shorebirds, pot-bellies wobbling
on wire legs.

I'm wishful like that. I used to pretend that the earth ended here.
Left at the truck stop, right at the scarecrow, past so much parched
corn that we seemed doomed. Then turquoise.

We'd cover our parents in sand, wear these maniacal grins. You
know, we pretty much became amphibians. I remember hearing,
from my bunk bed, the voices slacken with drink.

They're plastic. They never take on the cold of the lake, like they
don't know where they are? It was them versus my toy shovel, at
first.

There's a video: I'm freaking out, wearing the huge shirt I used to
hide puberty. More keep washing up. Whoever was filming me
blanked out on ethics, I guess.

Downstream, there's these places where boys don't get born. Ben
saw a cormorant regurgitate sunglasses. He wasn't stoned. We've all
sort of known each other forever.

Our parents won't believe him. So? They say to choose abstinence,
say to drive carefully, but to swim in a slow-motion catastrophe is
our birthright.

To let fake embryos surround our flip-flops. To build our fire,
cloaked in hoodies, hunched over clam-shells of pad thai. As big as
we want, like an inferno.

Higher With The Humidex

Evenings on the undivided
highways, hands in airstreams, everywhere fine
particles refracting.
The atmosphere

could mushroom from the west, percuss the windshield
and dissolve the view.

Some element of thunder
was in us. Or a moon of split bone

would rise on cables on a cornfield stage.

When I spoke it was meant
to make me seem from there, and failed
as fireworks extinguish.
Reeling

in the milk-crate lattice
of a truck, pink bristle skins

radiant with dusk. Proud
headquarters of, a wetlands
development by. The soundtrack

was hoarse guitars, someone singing darling,
don't you go and cut your hair.

Coda

So it goes. You grow strange as a park
I've only seen in winter,
laying bare the remains
of newspapers and cups. What it failed
to digest has turned to old news, will soon drown
in a barefoot flood that recalls
only its own green wake.

If I wanted less. If my want was as blank
as the fragment
of sky outside your room. You with your eyes
to a book while sleek
recurrent gulls raced past,
early longings I had meant
to lose, refusing.

The needle skips on a forgotten song
this morning, our bicycles
caught on the same corner. And we could hurl
questions like bricks,
but the light
starts to flash like a faltering heart,
an open palm saying   *look,   look,   look,*

I am coming up empty.

The Widows

They pull their groceries along in stuttering carts,
winded where

the street is steep. Their cardigan pockets
hold folded tissues, stashes of velvet tomato seeds:

Roman Candle, Moneymaker. In the shadows of houses, their gaze
is on remembered mountains, orchards fogged by cataracts.

The real sky, they sight it second-hand, when polishing their glasses.

There should be a word for a group of them, aligned on park benches,
square-heeled shoes scuffing the earth. They quarrel in the Romantic languages,

stay frugal even with feelings. Only the faded, plaster Madonnas know
the broken from the free.

In the evenings, to the clicks of bedroom lamps, the widows
grow enormous on the muted florals of their walls.

They soak their teeth, hang their tomorrows from the backs of chairs.

Pastorals in the Atrium

The tour has only started when
I'm ambushed by that flat-lined verdigris I'd know even
as a stumbling sleepwalker: *landschap*
with tin river, cleaver of sodden pastures —

marvellous for painters,
says the docent, was the enormity
of the sky, rarely cloudless, and she's already
turning to an Italian hillscape when I say wait! this is

my bloodstream, as my finger makes brief
unintended contact with the canvas,
and then my voice an ambulance
I tell her there should be a diagram
to indicate the grazing motion,
how the grinding molars of the Holsteins
make the river go —

or else, self-portrait
in the glassing-over eye
of a stickleback in a jam jar,
left too long in the sun —

but now the river is across the room because
the docent has ushered me towards an upholstered bench
and is murmuring, sit, sit, I have here from the staff-room
a coffee, here you are —

and I'm making the gesture for
no, those fields I ate and was made of
live in me, uncloseable
parentheses

January

Limestone buildings on limestone,
alkaline walls to scull
along as the porous body with a cold-soaked
coat, taped headphones.

No need to squint because
the sky is embedded with mortar
and fossils.

Red fox,
at the bottom of Cataraqui Street, where the mill was
and the tires in shrubbery are —
agile, shifty listener to its own brass solo,
taking such a generously unlinear while,
over the lake ice, to disappear.

Corridor

The train moves like a lit room through the night,
a constant minor quaking
of upholstery, vestigial ashtrays. Organ chords
sound out the liquid dark: it's bottomless. Bleary men
in overshoes, a teenager folded in sleep. Each wall
of windows holds a spectral train — their mirror interiors
scour the dark fields — as if the train
is conscious as a sea slug maybe is, and the hour
lets it risk these inklings of itself.

Snow lightens first, pooled in depressions, corduroy acres.
Rumble of iron at Napanee. Storm waters
over the dam. Field with spooked
deer-tail a fading smudge and there's
my face — when did a lag creep in, between how old
I imagine and am? A hot plate's singe
ignites the murk of coffee. Clapboard houses,
yard with an inflatable nativity, then plunge
of a river, scalloped with whitecaps.

That mauvish sunrise flooding idle fleets of trucks,
couch on frozen grass — photography
dilutes it, you have to soak your eyes. Rivulets of sumac,
upward bleeding ink. The suburbs have wave-form rooftops,
outskirts wrapped in Tyvek. Scrawled overpass:
an instant on another train, a passenger asks how
is gravity in my country — graffiti, he meant,
I got that too late.

Full daylight at Oshawa — voices muster, spirited thumbs
over phones. The train barrels in on a mild
decline. Each clanging cross-street
is a brick-walled gorge. It's early but too late.

Faces are hitched to their years. In crowds they deflect
what comes, or not, or not — minutes
when even other people stream in
as if benign, fiercely familiar.

Nocturne

From hawk to hawk
is how we drive
we sieve the sprawl
for what we love

The road unreels
and they appear
in perished trees
on post or wire

Lanterns on
each road we took
and take, remade
from hawk to hawk

Community Pool At Noon

Skylights, wadded
with dryer-lint clouds. Warm chamber
of pale tile that dampens
sirens and engines, blots the weekday
avenues to grays of pearl and shale —
here is azure.

Below the photo of the deceased
benefactor, his antique
rescue certificate. The water parts: pale dames
on noodles curved like sea-horses,
waterproof lipstick
and lashes.

In the lanes, two muscled adolescents
ricochet from wall to wall, and in the shallow end
a goggled, hemiplegic man keeps trying
to swim, but can't — ensnares
in the floating rope and hollers,
veers again.

I share his lane because
of how I move, fatigued and morning-sick.
He's a sad animal, flailing. Now I have to
love him, even. Dim lemon
lamps, rain weeping
over skylights —

from the archive,
chlorine lifts the swimming lesson: treading water
in an undulant one-piece, mildly asthmatic
and sucking in air
laced with vinegar pins, a fatherly
voice berating.

Pools are the same
in starkly different cities. Resumptions
of the fluid element, the skills
we keep refining: *Practical knowledge of rescue.*
Releasing oneself from the clutch
of the drowning.

Saint John

You say to the ocean, *we're here.*
Windshield frames the subdued sloshing
of the harbour. Chain link, guardhouse,

a cruise ship whiter than seagulls.
Salt and molluscs in our noses. Hours
down asphalt flanked with moose-fence,

thin coffee from lukewarm machines, for this
gray comforter, this wordless report
of mackerel and lantern fish,

remote, familiar strands. A man
in a windbreaker leans in your window
to ask, *where in Ontario?* He came here

to retire. Says *Sure was a good move.*
Scarborough's too full of — squints at me, sucks
down the words — *Your neighbours*

look out for you here. He nods his cap,
limps smaller in the sideview mirror.
The engine ticks. Your grin

is sore. I'm invulnerable, because
my hand is on my belly. Five months.
Kicking a jig, elated, without theory.

Neonatal

The nurses circled us like moons.
Your egg-shaped curve, my cradle arms.
We were two, still close to one,

and no one spoke our mother tongue —
the doctors swarmed,
the nurses circled, blank as moons.

Backlit saplings, your small lungs
— our cord was specimen, still warm —
we sudden two, closer to one,

milk-licked our wounds,
tuned out the rumour of alarms.
The nurses circled us like moon-

faced demons, lurking, hung
concoctions, weighed their harm.
I, the two reduced to one,

swept up our broken shell, clung
to your soft, curled form.
Nurses circled. Somewhere the moon
rose for the two of us, still close.

The New Father

Where are her bones? She's fog-eyed, all vowel —
rain could dissolve her.

Everything comes too close: exhaust,
the metallic, mirrored sky

— at night, the wail
under a transport's passing utterance —

even the praising hands
of strangers, even the neighbour's

sunflowers, their ravaged faces
turning to the earth.

This Be Our Verse

That was the creaking house where sunlight passed
as liquid clockwork over knotted floors.
It was either domestic or cosmic dust.
In small migrations we traversed the hours —

clockwork waltzes over knotted floors.
Speckled paper starlings flew
in small migrations. We traversed the hours
until morning, curtains turning lucid.

While paper starlings flew,
I searched under the furnace for your breath.
Mornings, I felt lucid until spoken to —
lulled by repetition: nurse, change, soothe.

Under the frugal tidals of your breath,
the quilted minutes folded out and in.
Nurse, change, soothe — along their thread
your progress was a kind of surfacing.

The quilted minutes folding out and in
like an accordion ballad from a park.
That first mirrored gesture: you surfacing
into your life. Common work.

Like that accordion ballad from the park
waltzing through the house where sunlight passed
into our liquid lives, our work.
We're so improbable. Dust is dust.

Dag en Nacht

A window from a window, amber square
where an artist works. I'm upstairs: she's a half-hidden
figure. My child wakes and wakes. The floor, pitched as a ship, splinters
minutely under my sway. An apron, hands moving over
a table — fevers shaping wire, paper, plaster. Once I think I saw her
string the heads of dolls together. Hammer dishes.

Maybe night's her only chance, maybe she sleeps into the pith
of day. Sleep! I want to sink in indigo fathoms,
anchors tied to my feet. Mornings are blinding
domes. Up the ice-rutted street I tell the stroller
what's what. We're almost neighbours, almost strangers:
birds in the woodcut, inverse forms of each other converged

over rivers and acres. Or the two circulations: systemic, pulmonary.
Or opposite shifts in the same factory.

Jesse's Farm

We're driving and the radio says mass marine extinctions within a generation. No silence, no sirens — an unflustered inflection, then stock markets, cryptic as Latin mass. I force myself: the interval between a mother and her child — not enough for refuge in numerics, reckoning we'll be old or gone. Her in my rear-view mirror when I skew it. Undoing velcro: velours crochet — the maker plucked burrs from his sweater, studied them under a microscope. There's a microscope I inherited, embedded in a fake snakeskin case. Ravaged scales, surges of herring with x's for eyes; already they're cartoons — I can't pretend because of her I should at least imagine them, the beaches I have known, putrid at low tide or maybe a dreadful, birdless quiet — but also I keep driving through commercial outskirts, dimly reading blowout signs. Her chirped naming: *excebator, earplane, cloud.*

We're going to Jesse's farm, which resembles the farms in our picture books. Ducklings hasten after lambs, pigs root in coffee-ground soil. Fences are makeshift there. Being from life, it isn't bloodless. A sow with a taste for chicks. The peacock, ornate as cabaret, reigning from the coop roof, lunging at what moves. *Almost there* — words half sung, but even my breast milk has an undertow.

So we're driving. Not with sirens. To the farm that resembles a refuge. Siren is the genus of the salamander eel. Sirenia, the order of the placid, grazing manatee. If I spoon-feed her the beloved world enough, is it?

Ravaged tides to picture. It isn't bloodless. Mirror, daughter, what will I wish that I did?

Which isn't what I say. *Hello old farm-gates, hello cedars.*

Here we are.

What Crows Say

Vendors of mornings, pitching
raucous, vernacular, lurching from lilacs
to eaves troughs, gurgling tuneful intimacies,
scolding cats, croaking elated
over crab apples —

kaa! dark glimmer in your pocketful of words

— some days, their calls bluster over
the stroller like proof: what I told you
is true. On others, the truth is them mutely
traversing the sky, bird-shaped holes
in the cloak of the world.

Lake Ontario Park

*P.S. You will Do well to try to Innoculate the Indians by
means of Blanketts, as well as to try Every other method that
can serve to Extirpate this Execrable Race.*

    - General Jeffery Amherst in a letter dated 16 July 1763

Over the warming ground, swings toll like clock tower bells.
Squirrels spiral the trunk of a pine.
We fill a pail with sand.
The day is robin's eggshell fine.

My mother's shoulder had three shallow scars.
Shining archipelago.
The quiet theatres of our lives.
Immune is a sung word, skirting sorrow.

Kneeling at no registry of toddlers with amorphous voices.
Night sweats without monument.
The lake has the sea on its breath.
One man has an island.

Picture Books

A caterpillar, tangent to the tissue paper earth.
Rabbits digging into carrot sandwiches.
Clean ovals of eggs in the chaotic straw.
The lamp wears the light like a skirt and the moon
is a pale coin we say goodnight to. Words
are still flotsam, crowding the edges, creaking.

Homemade little human: look. Later comes
with an upstream urge, a search for phrases
that return the lit world to us, never longer
than a flared instant. Even the words know it,
nailed together like makeshift furniture.
Stranded under the night sky, wanting to be lunar.

Yes,

I said. The wind
lifted the word and blew it
through the birches into smaller yesses
that dispersed.

Hitched bicycle ride, my hands
on your waist, soles skimming the road
in the bends.

What we wore will be one of those tellings
that even a latent, erasing disease
never steals. In tune like a robin and robin, a doorbell
and creak of the stairs.

Say love is the ship coming in.
Say the grave eyes of the birch trees
watched us go. How long

had we stood on the pier? Gulls squalled.
We'd outgrown what we packed.

Notes

"Strandbeesten" are the mobile beach creatures made by artist Theo Jansen.

The "Bloodbottler" is a character from Roald Dahl's book *The BFG*.

"I Am A Rock / What I Am" are the titles of songs by Paul Simon and Edie Brickell respectively.

"Because there was and there wasn't a city" is from artist Jamelie Hassan's work titled 'Because... there was and there wasn't a city of Baghdad'.

The lyrics cited at the end of "Higher With The Humidex" are from Stephen Malkmus' song 'Cut Your Hair'.

"Corridor" borrows its premise from the poem 'Afsluitdijk' by M. Vasalis. The first line is a translation of Vasalis' first line, except that the vehicle in the original is a bus.

"Dag and Nacht" is the title of a woodcut landscape by M.C. Escher.

The phrase "homemade little human" in the poem "Picture Books" is taken, somewhat altered, from Herman de Coninck's poem 'Poëzie'.

Acknowledgements

I'm deeply grateful to:

Each of you who gave me encouragement, spare hours, quiet rooms, or comments on drafts of the poems.

The editors of above/ground press, *The Antigonish Review*, *CV2*, *EnRoute Magazine*, *The Fiddlehead*, *Geist*, *The Literary Review of Canada*, *The Malahat Review*, *POETRY*, *Prairie Fire*, *This Magazine*, *The Best of Canadian Poetry in English 2008* (Tightrope Books), *Villanelles* (Everyman's Library), and CBC Radio, for publishing or broadcasting earlier versions of these poems.

The Ontario Arts Council and Canada Council for the Arts.

My editor, Ron Smith.

Sarah Tsiang & the Villanelles, Amy Rubin-Flett, Deborah Windell, J.C. Bellringer and Sarah B. Wiseman.

My parents and brothers.

Craig, thank you.

Anne-Marie Turza, grote blij.

Sadiqa de Meijer was born in Amsterdam, and moved to Canada as a child. Her poetry, short stories and essays have appeared in many journals, including *The Malahat Review*, *Geist*, *The Fiddlehead*, *Riddle Fence* and *Poetry Magazine*. Her poems were anthologized in *The Best of Canadian Poetry in English 2008* (Tightrope Books) and in the international anthology *Villanelles* (Everyman's Library). In 2012, her series "Great Aunt Unmarried" won the CBC Poetry Prize. She lives in Kingston with her family.